T0020389

All Families

Unhoused Families

by Annette M. Clayton

FOCUS READERS.

BEACON

www.focusreaders.com

Copyright © 2023 by Focus Readers®, Lake Elmo, MN 55042. All rights reserved. No part of this book may be reproduced or utilized in any form or by any means without written permission from the publisher.

Focus Readers is distributed by North Star Editions:
sales@northstareditions.com | 888-417-0195

Produced for Focus Readers by Red Line Editorial.

Photographs ©: iStockphoto, cover, 1, 14; Shutterstock Images, 4, 6, 8, 10, 13, 17, 19, 20–21, 22, 25, 27, 29

Library of Congress Cataloging-in-Publication Data
Names: Clayton, Annette M., author.
Title: Unhoused families / by Annette M. Clayton.
Description: Lake Elmo, MN : Focus Readers, [2023] | Series: All families |
    Includes index. | Audience: Grades 2-3
Identifiers: LCCN 2022030299 (print) | LCCN 2022030300 (ebook) | ISBN
    9781637394618 (hardcover) | ISBN 9781637394984 (paperback) | ISBN
    9781637395707 (ebook pdf) | ISBN 9781637395356 (hosted ebook)
Subjects: LCSH: Homeless families--Juvenile literature. |
    Families--Juvenile literature.
Classification: LCC HV4493 .C54 2023 (print) | LCC HV4493 (ebook) | DDC
    362.5/92--dc23/eng/20220815
LC record available at https://lccn.loc.gov/2022030299
LC ebook record available at https://lccn.loc.gov/2022030300

Printed in the United States of America
Mankato, MN
012023

About the Author

Annette M. Clayton is a writer and activist. She works to protect the environment and enjoys teaching kids about the fascinating world around them. She lives in Maryland with her twin daughters, husband, and one fluffy cat. For fun, she likes to read or go hiking.

Table of Contents

CHAPTER 1

Leaving Home 5

CHAPTER 2

Being Unhoused 9

CHAPTER 3

Challenges 15

MANY IDENTITIES

Homelessness and Race 20

CHAPTER 4

Differences at School 23

Focus on Unhoused Families • 28

Glossary • 30

To Learn More • 31

Index • 32

Leaving Home

The girl loves living in her family's apartment. Every night, she gets to sleep in her own bedroom. Her two brothers share another room. The girl's room is filled with fun toys. The kitchen has lots of good food.

 More than one in three US families rent their homes.

Sometimes courts order people out of their rented homes. This is called eviction.

The girl's dad has a job fixing cars. Her mom works at a hospital. Each morning, the girl goes to school.

One day, the girl's dad gets a letter. It's from the **landlord**. He says the price of **rent** is going up. But the family cannot afford the higher price. Soon, the landlord calls. He tells the family they must leave.

The family becomes unhoused. They sleep in a cheap motel. All five people share one small room. There is no kitchen. The girl misses their old apartment. But she still goes to school every day.

Did You Know?

Half of all unhoused children are five years old or younger.

Chapter 2

Being Unhoused

An unhoused family does not have a steady place to live. Many unhoused families stay indoors. Some families live in motels. Some live with family or friends. Others stay in **shelters** with other people.

 Hundreds of thousands of people stay in shelters every night in the United States.

 Unhoused people sometimes live together in encampments outside.

Some unhoused families do not stay indoors. They might not feel safe living in a shelter. Shelters have people they do not know. The family may sleep in their car.

Most families lose housing because of the cost. Parents might still earn money through work. But they might get paid too little.

There are other reasons that families become unhoused. For example, a parent might lose a job.

Did You Know?

In the United States, 1 in 16 people will face homelessness during their lifetime.

As a result, the family makes less money. Sometimes, there is extreme weather. Strong storms can damage homes. Families might not be able to pay for repairs. Other times, one parent is **abusive**. The other parent leaves with the children. It can be safer that way.

Some families are unhoused for a long time. It can last a year or more. However, most families are unhoused for a short time. It usually happens when there is a big

 The cost of rent often increases every year.

life change. This might be the price of rent going up. Or a parent might become ill. After a while, the family can pay for housing again.

Chapter 3

Challenges

Unhoused parents often work hard to make things as normal as possible for their kids. But leaving a home can still be very difficult. For example, the family might have to leave their neighbors.

 Saying goodbye to neighbors and friends can be very hard.

A family might also have less space than before. The family might need to leave some items behind. Children might leave behind their toys.

Shelters can have their own challenges. Many do not allow pets. So, some families have to find somewhere for their pets to go. Shelters can be also noisy. They are filled with strangers, too. Many people there are nice. But some might not be. Another challenge

 Lots of noise can make it hard to focus on homework.

is getting sick. In crowded places, germs spread more easily.

Everyday tasks can be harder, too. Some places don't have stoves. That makes it harder to cook meals.

Other places don't have washing machines. That makes it harder to keep clothes clean.

In addition, friends might not be able to come over. Spending time with friends is important. As a result, children might feel lonely.

Unhoused families can experience lots of emotions. Parents might

Did You Know?

Children without a home are twice as likely to get sick.

 It can be difficult for children to understand why their parents are feeling upset.

feel worried. They are working to

find a new home. Children often

notice when their parents are upset.

That might make the children feel

sad, too.

19

Homelessness and Race

People of color face higher homelessness **rates** than white people. For example, 13 percent of Americans are Black. But more than half of all unhoused families are Black. **Racism** is a major cause. Many landlords let fewer people of color rent. Police also charge Black people with crimes more often. That can make getting homes and jobs harder. Many people of color and white people have similar jobs. But employers often pay workers of color less. Low pay makes finding steady housing harder.

Black Americans face high rates of homelessness.

Chapter 4

Differences at School

Being unhoused can make school harder. For example, sometimes family members have to split up. Children might stay with grandparents. The parents might stay at a shelter.

 Leaving a parent is often very painful.

When that happens, children might miss their parents. That can make it more difficult to focus on school.

Unhoused families might not have enough to eat. Healthy food helps keep minds and bodies strong. It is tough to do homework while hungry.

People also need a good night's sleep. Crowded shelters can be very noisy. The noise can keep people awake. As a result, children might

 It can be hard to follow classroom rules when feelings are strong.

feel tired the next day. That also

makes it much harder to listen

at school.

Losing a home can be painful, too. Students might feel sad or angry. Those feelings make sense. Some children might want to talk about it. That can help **process** feelings. Others might not want to talk about it. Both responses are okay.

Unhoused children might live differently than other kids in their

Did You Know?

Families make up 30 percent of unhoused people.

 Talking with adults can help make hard feelings less scary.

class. They might miss a lot of school while they move. Some may need extra time with the teacher to learn. But differences are okay. It is important to be kind to everyone.

FOCUS ON
Unhoused Families

Write your answers on a separate piece of paper.

1. Write a sentence summarizing the main ideas of Chapter 2.

2. How do you think children in unhoused families should be treated at school? Why?

3. Where do some unhoused families stay?
   - A. houses they own
   - B. shelters
   - C. apartments they rent

4. What is one reason families can become unhoused?
   - A. Shelters become more common.
   - B. A parent becomes ill.
   - C. Housing costs are too low.

5. What does **extreme** mean in this book?

*Sometimes, there is **extreme** weather. Strong storms can damage homes.*

    A. safe

    B. always happening

    C. very powerful

6. What does **challenges** mean in this book?

*Shelters can have their own **challenges**. Many do not allow pets. So, some families have to find somewhere for their pets to go.*

    A. hard problems to solve

    B. places to stay

    C. animals to care for

Answer key on page 32.

Glossary

abusive
Violent or cruel.

landlord
A person or company that owns housing and receives payment from renters who stay there.

process
To think about something in order to better understand it.

racism
Hatred or mistreatment of people because of their skin color or ethnicity.

rates
Amounts of something when compared to something else. For example, suppose a town has 100 people. If 10 people in the town are unhoused, the town's homelessness rate would be 10 per 100 people.

rent
The amount of money people pay each month to live in a house or apartment.

shelters
Places, especially temporary ones, where people can stay when they have to leave their homes.

To Learn More

BOOKS

Davis, Raymie. *What Should We Do About Homelessness?* New York: Gareth Stevens Publishing, 2023.

Hyde, Natalie. *Housing and Homelessness.* New York: Crabtree Publishing, 2022.

Smith, Elliott. *Income Inequality and the Fight over Wealth Distribution.* Minneapolis: Lerner Publications, 2022.

NOTE TO EDUCATORS

Visit **www.focusreaders.com** to find lesson plans, activities, links, and other resources related to this title.

Index

A
apartments, 5, 7

F
feelings, 18–19, 25–26
food, 5, 24
friends, 9, 18

G
grandparents, 23

H
homework, 24

L
landlords, 6–7, 20

M
motels, 7, 9

N
neighbors, 15

P
parents, 11–13, 15, 18–19, 23–24

R
racism, 20
rent, 6, 13, 20

S
school, 6–7, 23–25, 27
shelters, 9–10, 16, 23–24
sickness, 17–18
sleep, 5, 7, 11, 24

T
teachers, 27

W
weather, 12

Answer Key: 1. Answers will vary; **2.** Answers will vary; **3.** B; **4.** B; **5.** C; **6.** A